CW01508860

A WILD GOOSE CHASE

Andrew McNeillie was born in 1946 in North Wales and brought up there, a son of the Scottish writer Ian Niall. After an unconventional start, he read English at Magdalen College, Oxford, before becoming a publisher and editor. For a key period in his life, he was literature editor at Oxford University Press. He is the founding editor of the magazine *Archipelago* (2007–) and runs the Clutag Press (now in its twenty-sixth year). His memoir *An Aran Keening* was published by the Lilliput Press, Dublin, in 2001, and reissued in 2025. *Once: A Memoir* came out from Seren in 2009. *Striking a Match in a Storm: New & Collected Poems* was published by Carcanet in 2022. A prequel to his Aran memoir, *News of the World: from Rhydamman to Inishmore* appeared from Lilliput in 2025.

A WILD GOOSE CHASE
ANDREW MCNEILLIE

CARCANET POETRY

First published in Great Britain in 2026 by
Carcanet
Main Library, The University of Manchester
Oxford Road, Manchester, M13 9PP
www.carcanet.co.uk

A CIP catalogue record for this book is
available from the British Library.

ISBN 978 1 80017 509 9

Book design by Andrew Latimer, Carcanet
Typesetting by LiteBook Prepress Services
Printed in Great Britain by SRP Ltd, Exeter, Devon

The publisher acknowledges financial
assistance from Arts Council England.

CONTENTS

In Memory of Richard Burton, 1956–2025

A WINDOW OF RAIN

Better early than late, I thought,
so as not to miss the boat.

Yet also better late than never,
late as it all is, now I am an old man.

I read the map in my head
contour by contour.

The map of November.
The place had its own words for

everything including me
as I stood outside, staring

at a window of rain
the day the rest of my life began.

IN THE WAKE OF PYTHEAS THE GREEK

1.

BEYOND THE PILLARS OF HERCULES

Outward I go
reading the stars,
and the sun
with my gnomon,
beyond the Pillars –
a new man
(after Thales),
throwing off
the old religion
of Ulysses & Co
and the gods
cutting through myth
with my prow.

Outward by
land and sea,
to Britain.
My story told in
On the Ocean
now lost, *maudit*
my Ultima Thule.
No copy surviving,
only quotation
and misquotation,
trashed by Strabo
(I ask you), but not by
Pliny or Hipparchus.

2. NOUS

Think of yourself in his shoes
or whatever he wore on his feet.

Think what it was like to be Greek,
4th-century BC, and not Greek.

Think of him and his retinue
saying how-do-you-do

to sailors and traders
at primitive harbours

spinning yarns. Comparing notes
about sea-roads and boats.

Tracing word-of-mouth
to the horse's mouth.

Reaching the fabled source of tin.
And on to Llŷn, Mona, Man.

Brokering passage between
wild tribes. Waiting about in

the cold. (Think of the rain
tipping down.)

Think of it hour by hour,
at sea or ashore.

To Stornoway and the 'forty'
isles of Orkney.

A trading man of learning and science.
A man of resilience.

Pytheas the intrepid, and mysterious.
A man of vision and *nous*.

3. PERI TOU OKEANOU (ON THE OCEAN)

In leaps and bounds, a deer in the mountains,
dashing from the hunt, dashing like a fish
in the side of a wave, chased by the winds,
in hail and lightning, winging it between notes.
Think of a currach, storm-tossed, off Inis Mór,
no more than lath and canvas between you
and your maker, pitching close to perpendicular.
Poseidon with his trusty trident never had
such seas up his sleeve in the *Odyssey*.
Never did the Med see the like, sea-soaring,
see-sawing, peak and trough. Now haul hard
on raw ropes, going, and going about,
to hold high ground, clear of foundering glens –
a pod of dolphin; a sea-bird throw of the dice,
in the lemon skies of dawn; and heather-banked,
in the hush and rush cacophony of storm,
black and livid, whorling, heeling, hurling,
bottle-green, glittering-green, aerated spate –
with azure and coral-strand interludes,
in the Hebrides, by Mediterranean colourists –
schooling his heart as it sails off the chart,
extending the reach clear to the Arctic
of every wilful mind. Arriving, arriving –
outward to somewhere behind the North wind,
measuring the sun's height at the solstice,
calculating, within a whisker of true,
the perimeter of the Island of Britain,
founding what we know of the archipelago.
Scanning the horizon from Hermaness Hill,
to start a hare running on Ultima Thule.

4. AT HERMANESS (SHETLAND ISLES)

A lark on the strand, a man in the gap.
Whoopers arrowing North,
trumpeting. The brass air
burnished with cold.

Ice-cold the breeze about him.
A congealed sea, they called it,
up there on the migratory arc
to Rifstangi and the Arctic.

Navigate by sea-bird and star,
rain-taste and merest breath of air.
He's learnt a language since,
he hadn't known before.

Like a lark on the strand.
Now there he stood and thought,
weighing things up
as you would, in his shoes.

5. THULE

What would the language have been there
in c. 320BC? Supposing he braved it.
Were the Irish there before Christ?
Or just the intertribal trading set?
Cod fishermen in hide canoes with square sails?
See what you prefer. Believe what you hear.

In the Circle of the Bear the one-eyed
dome of light is king, opaque as jellyfish,
refracted mirage, from *jökull* to *ísjakanum*.
But what words for them then?
And where? And how far away?
See what you believe. Believe what you see.

6. PALIMPSEST

Gather at the old harbour, in Marseille,
where he's figured on the facade of the Bourse
(*music off*: 'La Marseillaise'), and hail him,
however he came, from 'Abalus', with
the origin of amber traced, to some bleak
North Sea or Baltic tideline; or from 'Kantion',
with only word-of-mouth for proof.
However he made it, don't side with those who say
he made it up, the sneering snobs
of Greece and Rome. We all know their kind.
They have never gone away.
But gather now to honour him. Attend
like Hipparchus, scrolling down the papyrus
line by line of a copy of a copy,
reading there with latitude in mind.
The great astronomer of Rhodes
in his debt; and, if so, surely we are.
Embark in his footsteps if you think you can
disinter them from the palimpsest,
look for a boat across the channel.
(Observe the latter-day voyagers
at their peril.) Trail-blaze to old knowledge.
Visit the tin mines, and the metal market
on St Michael's Mount. Stay out all night
half-starved on the heath, until you start
to hallucinate. Then believe what you see:
the shade of Pytheas, star-gazing on a promontory.
Go pre-Socratic. Re-establish Nature.
Play the method actor. Soliloquise
on Porthcurno's stage, above the Atlantic,
and tread the boards of our tragedy.

Think of yourself in his shoes as you go,
hugging the coast, keeping your notes.
And see if, left to your own devices,
you can't reckon the height of the sun
on midsummer's day. Survey the Northern world
of shrinking ice, where the Plough
shares the crown with the Bear
and will long after there's no ice there.
Be chastened by what's befallen his original:
Earth's miracle, still hanging on for now.

7. BURNT OFFERING (RHODES, SUMMER 2023)

The fires rage. Engulfed in his observatory, Hipparchus can go nowhere. At night the island glows with fingers of fire like tributaries of lava. If it was his turn to sleep the airless heat and drone of water-bombing planes would wake him.

He sticks to his latest task: numbering space debris, pausing only to wipe ash and smut from his lens, sweat from his brow. So far he's reached 23,000 pieces this week.

In downtime, he takes from its shelf his copy of a copy of *Peri tou Okeanou*. He calls it his comforter. It reminds him how once he was the first to catalogue the stars, when mystery and wonder still possessed the world.

TIME ALONE

Make a start. Don't say a fresh one.
Just step out. Let what you enter
do the rest. Learn not to resist.
The clean sea-light on land and
water, your element. Accept its way
of showing, not how but now,
the duck-rabbit coastline.

Make a start, suspend thought.
Don't unfold the map.
Set all names for places
and creatures aside. Follow
the tide. Switch off.
Let Earth wrap you in its warp.
Immerse yourself in time alone.

Then when you get home
don't try to write it down
as if to keep it for the future.
Don't burden it. See that
what you saw was of the hour
and needs no other measure,
unless it chooses to return your visit.

I sit in a corner at a table, my stick
leaning against the wall.
The place is empty but for me.
It is a perfect Tuesday morning
bright after a night's rain.
I have an upright drink before me
ready to let down,
and a book I'm reading
about a place not far from here.

Bucket and mop in hand, the landlady
throws open the door.
The bucket grates on the street.
The mop slops and slaps as,
stooping, back she steps, stretching
to reach under bench and table,
now mopping at my feet,
for me to pick them up and
set them down when she's done.

My drink makes room
for another. And as I wait
at the counter I hear
the gutturals of a trawler
and see a wheelhouse
glide by the window.
The day is casting off,
and so am I, happily
under way writing this
somewhere in my head as I read.

The bar begins to fill,
the talk to rise and fall
like the tide that waits on no one
for a word in edge-ways.
I drain my glass, and,
reaching for my stick
to keep me steady,
edge my way out, unsteadily,
saying, unnoticed: 'Thanks very much'
and 'Goodbye.'

A WORLD APART

Here they come, round the point,
the first boatload of the day,
trailing a few gulls. Inaudible,
the little cacophony of a crowd,
excited to catch the moment of arrival
in a world apart, gazing,
and pointing their cameras.

What is this for? It keeps the place afloat,
the fragile *indigène*,
as you'll make out
if you stay the night,
to sleep and wake in
the sound-warp of the island,
its mother tongue and weather.

Now, when morning breaks
and the first boat labours in,
on a Force 8, go down to watch
the next crowd disembark,
looking queasy and pale.
Lean on the wall. Stare
into the distance as they pass.

That's how I used to play it when
the first pilgrims stepped ashore
to herald Spring –
in their anoraks and plastic macs,
paying homage in the rain
at fort and clochán and shrine,
weeks before the corncrake came.

THE LOOP

As when I stepped ashore, the motion of the sea
still on me, and the world turning
under me, and the folk on the quay
down for their supplies staring at
an strainséir, looking so green, in the November evening.
The air in the shelter of the bay
black as the sea and steeped in brine.

No one to meet me until McDonough
who'd ignored me up to then
asked was I going where I was going.
I said I hoped to be, and he said,
'I'm here to meet you, come with me.'
And off we drove in his blue pick-up
with old Maggie Feaney in the back

among the Calor Gas cylinders
while we rode warm and dry in the cab
winding the rainswept way uphill,
into the shrouds of fallen clouds.
The only thing in common with now:
how I had no idea, when I began,
where I might go with my pen.

And here I am in the loop
from which it seems there's no escape.
Not that there weren't loops then
on the road that travels the island,
from end to end, bound
by the sea and the heavens.
Only I hadn't found them.

Only I hadn't seen how time works.
Or understood the simple laws.
How memory builds its house
as you must slate a roof from
the bottom up while a poem
is built from the top down
with no idea when it will reach the ground.

OLD MAN

The thing is, now, I go there any time.
I don't even have to leave home.

Which is as well as I'd find it beyond me,
clambering those rocks, to reach the sea.

I go where I go by memory solely.
It limits me, surely.

But there are blessings to count.
It's so much easier to get about.

In a moment I might be anywhere,
or wherever I've been before.

And with anyone I've ever known
and no one can tell where I am or when.

Or understand how they can't begin
to compete for my attention.

A WILD GOOSE CHASE

A
wild
goose chase
was once a horse race
and a tactic to keep the lead in a skein
of runners and riders, a sharp-elbowed strategy
for seeing off the field, now lost in the mists of time.

And
nothing
to do with arrowing
migrations, or tarred feet
on the road to market, or that hiding to nothing
writing poems can seem, as they cross the page to whiffle down
and gab away amid the alien corn, to hold the hour against the race of time.

SEIZE THE DAY

1. *Latitude*
I found today where I expected it to be:
everywhere, hereabouts, all day.

The same the world over I suppose
as Earth rides its wave, where dark and light

chase each other in and out of house
and home, and someone's breakfast

is another's supper, lit by Venus,
given food on the table, and chance to notice.

As time and the sea ravel and unravel –
from light to dark and dark to light.

2. *Longitude*
Arrival and farewell of wild geese,
North and South turn-about.

Between native Greenland
and the stubbled farmland.

Their gaggle and gabble true to
tradition. Nothing punctual

but in good time, though
seasons lose their way between.

Seize the day all seem to say
and so I try (while stocks last).

SAFE HAVEN

I stayed a few nights
to walk the old haunts
that have ghosted my life ever since.
It could only be dream-like
my once-upon-a-time
had been so potent.

It was as if I'd never known
anywhere else, wherever
I'd travelled in-between.
The way things were
and what might have been.
I call it my mooring.

The submerged bedrock
below the tideline
of appearances.
The place to take my bearings from
no matter where I am
when the time comes.

LUCK

The catch swings aboard, quicksilver spilling.
Shoal and sea go on their way

invisibly repaired
a net slipping away into night.

The fish chase their hunger.
I shoot for them, deeper.

Far shore-lights blink and waver
off somewhere I remember as

here, where I go plunging down
between the sheets, hoping that

when I wake and reach in the dark for the light
at 4 a.m. my luck will try me again.

THE SPEED OF LIGHT

I'm nearing the point in life
where all is dream-like
and seeming visionary.
No, I'm not in poor health
though I can't walk
as far as I'd like to.

I need more shrines
than any pilgrim on
the mountain path
ever paused to pray at.
I can no longer reach
the lifeboat station.

Forget the fisher's rock that
these days would
topple me into the ocean.
Which I'd rather not
if you please
however well the thought

reminds me of the island
and the pulse of Blind Sound
where I saw how
poems begin far from themselves
then travel at the speed of light
once they've a mind to.

DEAR EVENING

An old man watches his reflection grow
in the glass before him and the gleam
die before his eyes, in a darkening horizon
of seabirds and waves, signs to read
through blot and smudge of stormy weather,
a lifetime in the moment's spectacle.
A gale about the house, timbers creaking
in the roof. The island standing its ground.
And the whole thing an act of memory.

'Dear Evening,' his reply, peering into
the mirrored light, out beyond
his reflection, where allurements meet
in brief epiphany: the numen that
pervades the soul, as by divine order,
the fugitives 'here' and 'now' caught,
where nib touches paper, as his pen
crosses the page from port to starboard,
seeking words for joy-in-sorrow.

'Dear Evening, host of melancholy,'
he writes, 'all-season mood-swinger,
but most in winter, when you steal up on
the light, and linger, outwaiting
in mind, in storm-lit monochrome,
flinging sea-birds through the air and
sea-spray in flecks and flashes, splashes
where rocks blacken, maps of lichen
lose outline, and skylines sharpen.

Things as spare as words should be.
So ascetic November recruits me
to your staring-match with night,
no matter you'll blink first,
as shadows rise, into the cosmos,
and all the world turns black as ink.
To leave me hearing the wind
in the chimney; rattling at
door and window, trying to get in.'

THE GOOD LORD

A god of my appointing –
a stone from an island.

Dome-shaped like the Ailsa Craig
my doorstep *lare* or Lord.

A mitre laced with lichen
from some ancient religion.

All our observances are open air
with neither hymn nor prayer.

Were he to speak he would say
I put words in his mouth.

'LOCH SCAVAIG FROM ELGOL' BY JASON HICKLIN

Only art can silence the island's vast sound-warp
and stem the weather's tide
as it turns from flood to ebb
and light exchanges glances with itself
to the last moment of making.

Ourselves the one thing not indifferent
to our being here, as we pass through
the lighted island. What we bring
and what we take away
always something else and other.

Just so, as now, gazing at 'Loch Scavaig from Elgol'
I pass through the lighted gallery
in very different weather.

The Shipping Forecast's litany
his lullaby, he sails into sleep
above Morocco Street:
his mind as filled with poets
as Bass Rock with gannets.

> *... warnings of gales in Plymouth Biscay*
> *Fitzroy Sole Hebrides Faroes...*

Sails above his ink-black
engine-room, over the depths
and shadows of presses
plates and papers
dreaming of islands and wild places.

> *Out Stack Muckle Flugga Papa Stour Foula*
> *Cape Wrath North Rona St Kilda*

Adrift on sleep's high seas
above his studio where
prints on paper from Japan
or Korea hang
drying like fish in a smokehouse.

> *Boreray Flannan Barra Head Tory Malin*
> *Inishturk Inishshark Inishbofin*

Startled awake, he minds
the gap between his bed
and High Island, as the sea
waltzes, and stumbles,
among sea-birds and seals.

> *Inis Mór The Cliffs of Moher*
> *Black Head The Flaggy Shore*

Until he sinks back, on course
for morning again
and the darg of his vision
after coffee and a cigarette
on his roof-top terrace.
                    Blaskets Skelligs Scarrif
                    Deenish and Dursey

As the rush-hour floods
over London Bridge, into the City,
hard by the glittering Stac
of the Shard. Until it's time
to go below and make a work of art.
                    … warnings of gales in Plymouth Biscay
                    Fitzroy Sole Hebrides Faroes…

WAVING

I cut my losses, or so I thought,
but they snagged my keel
and slowed me down,
though sometimes it seemed
I was getting away.

Towards a fresh start,
whatever that might be.
At least, now, I could find out.
But as I sailed on, the island only
loomed nearer behind me.

Until it was as if I was still there
down on the quay
both waving myself off
and waving back
from the boat I was on.

YOU ARE HERE

Let's say, it's as if you're out walking.
You find yourself lost, with only
the map of memory for guide.
The four winds gust under it,
and over it, making it flap – like a sail
when a boat goes about,
or a kite on the end of a string
corkscrewing wildly, hellbent
on plunging into the ground –
never for a moment still, with you
stopped in your tracks, distressed
by loss and sorrow, searching
for a sign that would mean 'You are here',
insofar as you could be
and ever be made whole.

AT LIZARD POINT

This summer afternoon is all *plein air-*
pleine mer seascape light, playing on shifting surfaces
of blue-green gauzy semi-transparency
and white of sail and hull, and gull
and crest, and broken waves about
skerry and cove where families go,
to play and bathe, a time to itself, and
nothing beyond it, but a haze of horizon,
and the whole of England at its back,
forgotten, at least for the afternoon.

Only the blank gaze of Fonnereau's lighthouse
might disturb the moment's ease,
and prompt thought. Why is it there
and what is it for? – a word to the wise,
were we to pause, to rock the boat
above old wrecks where men
are fishing 'The Graveyard of Ships'
and mariners, in perfect conditions.
This afternoon no one wants to think
anything much, but dream and relax.

They stake a claim to a little turf, a corner
by the rocks, to watch nothing happen
but the changing light, their kids at play,
surf barely a whisper or a splash, their eyes
narrowed by the sparkling sun's jopling and jinking.
Shallows are our medium today, not depths.
Folk come and go to kiosk and café.

Their dogs pant, too hot to bark, and lap
a dazzling bowl. Their ice-cream offspring
have gone to heaven without knowing.

I watch two lovers come up the steep lane
from the shore, transported like Iseult
and Tristan, hooked on some potion,
and maybe they are doomed to tragedy
but it doesn't look like that today,
happy as they are, loitering to embrace,
dawdling along. He kisses the nape of her neck.
Then on they go away from the sunset
as the exodus inland begins of bickering brats
ready for bed and frazzled parents.
The kind of scene I don't want to be in.

I pass them all as I go down to the shore.
KILLJOY WOZ HERE I write in the sand
with my stick and linger towards the tide's
retreating edge, wondering if it ebbs
much farther whether I'll get to see inside
Davy Jones's Locker, and who will be first
to greet me if I do? A drummer boy
from the Peninsular War? Sole survivor
of *HMS Primrose*. Did he cling to his drum?
Did it float him ashore in the cove?
Did he live to fall in love with a girl?

Did he kiss the nape of her neck on
a summer afternoon? The air cools.
The tide seems about to turn. Still they come,
staring and mouthing who knows what,

in what dialect of sorrow? I guess
from his dress this one must be Lord Belhaven,
pondering an irony, en route to govern
the Barbados aboard the ill-fated *Royal Anne*
in 1721 and the Age of Slavery.
But what odds does it make to know?

Why do I let it get to me, this pointless life?
The useless past, this disconnection?
Summon up from the deep who or what
I might, what difference does it make?
To tell how we got to where we are
and how we did not, by what collateral,
what personal tragedy, what loss and grief?
Some difference to know more, some
to know less. I want what I know to
adjust my line of thought and hold what's
here and now in reverence and wonder.

Coda

I stood on there, almost to the last of light,
and the tide began to lap my feet
when a shade approached me from behind.
I didn't startle, though the waders rose
and sped away piping in alarm. I knew him
without looking. 'Hilary Chandler,' I said.
'Yes,' came his answer, 'we never met,
but my widow gave you things of mine:
a compass, feathered hooks, a bleached
wood frame and mackerel line…'
'I have them still,' I said, 'for remembrance.

'A material elegy, to keep your name above
the waves: the charts you drew of hotspots,
the main bass run at flood tide, marks
to heed between Maen Chynoweth and
Sharks Fin, hazards round the Manacles,
rocks and wrecks, location you put
to *Primrose*, *Mohegan*, *Juno*, and advice:
to recce first at low spring tide
(worth heeding more generally in life).
So, staring into the dark, at Lizard Point,
I restore you, to the spirit of this place,
to make a difference, here, if nowhere else.'

SINGING SCHOOL

I was sitting on a balcony by the sea,
quite early one morning,
sipping a *mocha* –
wondering idly
about Melville's hyphen
and what it might mean,
there as it was,
like me, in-between.

Moby-Dick on the table
beside me, a polar wind
blowing through it. Not
to be taken up lightly.
An old copy on near-Bible paper,
a Bible in itself, opening
the history of the Planet,
dwarfing all philosophies before it...
as Emerson dreamed.

The Last Day of the *Pequod*
if not of Moby Dick himself
voyaging in perpetuity
to circumnavigate the world
the moment the ink dried
and FINIS was the word
to cast off from,
to sail the allegorical sea
between evil and good.

Now outside its pages,
no one around to sing
Jonah's canticle
to a pantomime God.
No survivor to say
'Call me Ishmael'.
From pole to pole
another tale has seized the day:
of Whale-kind, their songs,
and singing school.

Mocha – a pun, here, on the white whale of oral tradition, 'Mocha Dick'.

WE SAD STRAGGLERS

It is November's eve and the dark is gathering
its farewell to light. At the bottom of the garden
a blackbird feeds in the branches of a rowan,
pecking at straggling berries for its wintering.

In endless harvest the sea threshes silver straw,
flailing wildly. The season asks no one to forgive
its intrusion as it goes from door to door.

Still, as one door closes another opens. Last orders
called at eight in the morning. O how I remember
that rude awakening into winter's
blurred light, down the sea-road from October.

The ferry aglitter at the pier-head and the others
there to wave goodbye to we sad stragglers.

THE SCENE OF MY UNDOING, ALL OVER AGAIN

I drew a line *Latitude 53° 07´* with my ruler
from November to October.
A clean line I thought
like a break with the past.
Then I stood back.
A line under what?
Too much to keep out.

Here I go, I said to myself,
all over again, in-between
W. Longitude 9° 50´ and *37´* –
minutes like me that don't move on
with *45* bisecting the bay
where I'd like my ashes strewn
at highwater one day.

Where wintering waders
pipe and scatter
and in spring the lark continuously singing
climbs from haven to heaven –
to stoop and loop in silence down again
as I revisit the scene
of my undoing.

And in the month of June
do I need to say
the corncrake's asymmetry
and the one-eyed *cimetière marin*
blowing forever
to the echo of hooves and waves
in that eavesdropping time.

Time from November to October
that so possesses me still,
surely there must be
something wrong with me?
O come to my rescue if you will.
You have the coordinates.
And may you find me soon,
there or here, I don't mind.

NATURE & ME

No, I said, I'm not here,
doing my bit, best I can,
to be close to Nature
but to those times when
there was no such thing to me
outside the dictionary.

I mean when I was in my element
out in the elements
and my thoughts were seamless,
reversible against the flow
of irreversible time.
And my nights the same

when I slept with them
wheeling about me
as I plunged towards day
as I would step with them
knowing and being
what I saw and heard

in my mother tongue
and no need to translate
as I spoke or ask the word
for corncrake, for example,
when wooed by one
crexing round my brain.

And the breeze billowing
my curtain and the sea
drawling towards high tide

as on those nights
I'd keep it company
and help haul it aboard.

The reversible tide
enlarging everything
into the galaxies
and me in my only clothes
sheltering from squalls
against harbour walls.

All at first hand and
drying out quick
as limestone in the wind
or at my hearth
as the storm rained and
stars hissed in the chimney

like hailstones. Or
is that not what you meant?
I have an inventory of trespasses.
A species count
if that's what you want
and a solemn thought

to shadow the story.
Forgive me but I'm only
saying how it was once
and not that long ago
when I was part of Nature
and it was part of me.

HOMELESS

'Dispossession is also nine-tenths of the law,'
I heard myself say, as if someone was there.
But ask the homeless and hear them wonder,
'What happens to the other tenth?'
It gets turned into words, for worse or better.

MEMORY PUZZLE

The picture on the lid's too faded
to make out exactly what should be where
though still more helpful than
recollection's certainties.

And here are the pieces in the box
of which also many are missing,
including the roof of the house
now left   as you see

       open

      to the wax table-cloth

        beneath.

There are   in the sea
     holes
and most of the gannets are
              missing.

The ferry on the horizon has either

              sailed away

or sunk.

It seems a stretch of cliff has
        f
      a
      l
      l
        e
         n

          into the ocean.

The curlews are gone

                   and the mackerel

      with them.

Some pieces fit nowhere at all, like

                            blow-ins

from another scene.

It's a puzzle all right
but what I can say is,
it's closer to reality now
than the original ever was.

HERE AND NOW

for Julian Bell and Garry MacKenzie

How many dimensions of now
can I snatch from the air,
in this stark space, more than linear,
where we see the poem we hear –
three dimensional as it is, to show
or tell (and both at once), to give
the illusion of being just what it is
and nothing left out, and never
to shift its ground, whatever happens
in time's hinterlands?
                              Never to vanish
into thin air, as the skein of geese
that stopped my heart disappeared
into its future, to gaggle down
on stubbles at nightfall far from here
in a chorus of call-notes I remember
as winter closes in on autumn
with imperfect timing, between here
and the shrinking Arctic Circle.
How many? Always too few.

I.M. CNUT

Now on the sea-road shore, you see a scar
where trucks dumped boulders and
high-viz workmen in the rain, with
long-handled shovels and tar, tidied up
the potholed lane, rebuilt the drystone
tumbled by the tide, expert at repair.

But forget this one, I remember the last time
I made it there, to lean on my stick a while,
staring at the sea, bewildered, internalising
the damage I saw, comparing the extent of it
with the previous one's devastations
and wondering how it would all end.

SATURDAY NIGHT

I can hear the sea break, close
to high-tide, and a horse's hooves,
cart-rims grinding at the turn.
Tonight the speed of sound is
steady as light from stars.

Step and set whoop through the years
and the week lets down its hair.
Hooves again and the real go-round
of alcohol, hormone, romance.
I can see and hear it from here.

How airless it was in the hall,
the crowd dancing towards midnight –
watchers glass in hand at the wall
or pissing their horse-stale outside,
music carrying to the ebbing tide

to die away in the dark
as the small hours began to unreel
towards the first of day
no one can remember greeting
or where it found them sleeping.

Still dancing, the Atlantic
whelms round them.
The tide falls.
The tide climbs.
A lost soul wakes in another's arms.

NOT AT HOME

In what sense was I there?
I mean in those everyday
absorbing island days with
their osmotic rhythms
and needs-must make ends meet,
the archetypal stranger.

Ever since I left there
and going back when I can
to stop it leaving me behind –
as, short-changed by change,
it takes leave of itself –
we both seem to cling on.

If escape is involved
it draws no line between
'to' and 'from'. Round I go
in ritual remembrance now:
embarking and disembarking,
as if according to

the ferryman's duty roster.
It does no harm to anyone unless to me.
I prefer rough seas to calm
but there are days still when
weather permitting applies
and poems are cancelled.

Then I hear the Atlantic
ransack my brain
and squalls of rain

pelt me as they used to
rattle and slatter down till
now I drown to recall

a deluge hemming the world in
and holding it away,
with me in-between, waiting.
. If I learnt anything there
it was to wait things out.
No matter where I am

. stranded, these days,
in the waiting game,
I have some expertise
to draw on, schooled
as I lived minute by minute
in that time there.

So what, if this is where
. I've ended up and say
it's where I live and
if where you live is home
then I'm home where
I'm not at home?

At home to anyone
calling round but
at heart somewhere else,
not where our eyes meet
and so it has been for
longer than I can remember.

THE RULES OF THE GAME

I often wonder what it would be like
to be grounded in memories of Mass,
and ritual, Salvation's rigmarole.
To have been an Altar boy, to know
the touch of the wafer on my tongue,
the metallic tang of blood in wine.
To fear Hell and trace the sign of the Cross
on my breast, to kneel in prayer,
and disappear into a world apart
where history speaks Roman Catholic.
To accept the Priest's authority,
or at least to go along with it, in case,
keeping my thoughts to myself.
To have whispered through the little grille
'Forgive me, Father...' and be forgiven
for the price of a few Hail Marys.
Then to step out onto the road
with the other men I've known
since childhood, cracking jokes,
parting for home, or on to the pub
for the match on the box, and me
knowing the rules of the game,
and the teams, as well as the next man.

TRAVEL LITERATURE

1.
I wait in the library
for my request to arrive.
Light concentrates
about a murmuring silence
and a rattle of keyboards
like mice behind the skirting.
What are they writing?

Someone, a revenant,
far from the long past
installs herself near me,
her chair scraping
and knocking at the desk
as she draws herself in,
throws back her hair,
consults her phone,
then begins her devotions
in the dark wood
of knowledge-in-waiting.

2.
My mind wanders.
I look about. I look at the sky
as leaden today as nearby
dome and roof.
I wander in my mind.

3.
Curlew in the rain, skittish as ever,
a rarity now, give my game away
as I try to step in, seamlessly,

fishing upstream against the flow.
I mean the flow of time.

God bless the right to roam
and the art of waiting.
Mind-travel like all travel
but freer and more agile
until it comes to writing.

4.
Here comes Thomas Pennant
up from the stacks at last.
I want to check my memory
against his.
Two memories, his and mine.

The sum total of our forgetting
an enticement to pause
and look up again,
gazing inward at somewhere
between picturesque and commonweal.

What goes into making a place
goes into making this. Nothing definitive.
The library about me
feels the weight of light.
A now sustained by concentration.

But at Llanddwyn? He and I
saw a world, and worlds apart.
The best a reader can do –
hold one world up to another
to spark imagination.

The tide comes in and breaks
against the causeway.
I have found what I wasn't looking for.
It is a eureka moment
soon to leave me behind.

The effect, as I remember,
startling. Oyster-catchers
piped into flight.
Their notes now as soundless
as the mountains beyond the strait.

5.
I look up again. I'm
not cut out for this business,
mood-driven, restless.
I deflect from words
as skittish as a curlew.

I see from the spines of her books
my neighbour's 'field'
is Romanticism.
The true sublime
at the birth of the machine.

You can still hear the wheels turning
as the book-trolley
comes round. Books
the baseline here,
going nowhere, going everywhere.

They thrive on paradox
like philosophers.
To prove you can be

in two places at once,
open the book of your choice.

I read in mine and pray.
How often may we
fall into grace?
As rarely as possible
to make the deepest sense.

6.
Now I take the zig-zag path
I knew in youth,
the perfect figure
for this to-fro enterprise
between then and now.

Thither and hither to follow him
up through Gloddaeth
to the summit
of touristic delight,
the panorama west towards the strait.

The summit of my everyday
once, and commonweal.
Embattled Creuddyn grown
wild with settlement since,
trashed, Pennant might have said.

Though 'modish rectitude'
was not for him. But breathtaking still
the windswept bryn
above the town above Wales,
over and above the half-moon bay.

'The Conwy pouring into
the Irish Sea,' as he said.
Home turf. Here I meet him.
I touch his page
with an index finger

like a child learning his letters
parting rare plant-names
from the Latin
as once my young hands parted
rough grasses in the karst

to find speedwell, cranesbill,
madder, cinquefoil, gentian.
Now surviving here in print
and memory, granted
a moment's grace.

A sharp taste, piquant sensation,
a kind of synaesthesia
among bowed heads
lost between book and screen.
My neighbour half-way up Yr Wyddfa

I like to think or
maybe in Cambridge or Paris.
About her travels anyway
with no idea where they might lead
or when they'll revisit her

however many years later.
I begin to up sticks and leave
quietly, as if invisibly,
leaving my books
at the counter marked returns.

ORME'S HEAD

(i)

The downfall of the father of St Tudno,
the drunkard Seithenyn of the feeble mind

who slept on his watch and let the tide
drown the kingdom of Gwyddno

when life was mythical and mystical –
might prove a timely parable

in the annals of climate disaster,
rising sea and melting glacier.

(ii)

I remember in youth dreaming of a tide
high enough to encircle the Orme's Head.

And cut it off into insular allure
and mystery, a hard place to make landfall.

A rich karstland off our coastline
where the descendants of those stranded there

kept sheep and ferried them to market
in late summer and early spring,

spoke the purest Welsh ever heard
and filled St Tudno's church with song.

(iii)
I waited and I watched the waters
but saw my prayers go unanswered.

I saw reality hold its ground and progress ride
roughshod over the world.

Over my mind, my island headland,
in all its disrepair and native sorrow.

Its wilful idyll nowhere near
yet never far from seeming real.

(iv)
Now, as the turbines turn in the sun
and glint as they labour in the fields of light

I ride the tram to the summit,
scanning horizons of sea and mountain.

Time in outline's timeless; but not
now and here, in the heart's winding shed

where the sins of the fathers go round
by the winding-sheet of the sea.

(v)
I remember, I say, but it's only a memory.
The least reliable faculty.

I remember better times in a girl's arms
above Happy Valley, before now turned to then.

Before now looked for help, unable
any more to fend for itself.

To undo what's done. To find somewhere to live
where life might do more than hold on.

Not only where but how. As the story says
St Tudno did despite the sins of his father.

ORME'S HEAD II

Latecomer

They wouldn't let me go to his funeral:
they thought at twelve I was too young.
But it wasn't then things started to go wrong,
that had set in long before my arrival.

They lowered him in next to Jean McDougall,
grandma as I knew her, who'd died not so long before,
far from Govan, where she first saw
the light, long before my arrival.

Now there they lay together, their struggle
over; two stories out of nowhere back together,
buried on the Great Orme, aligned with the Machair,
where he was born, long before my arrival

when a boy might go to such a funeral –
long before their world started to unravel,
displacing the never-quite-happy couple
South in search of work. Yet they lived well

enough at last, if wearing thin, half-way up a hill,
on a rocky lane, above the Irish Sea,
closer to home but still too far away for me,
wanting as I did to have things brought full circle.

The fabled circle that never could include me
but left me outside, long before my arrival;
and now, long after, finds me searching the cemetery
for a headstone, like a latecomer at his own funeral.

O the March Hare! The Hare!
Poussie McLièvre…

I lie in bed, waking slowly.
Light leaks in at curtain and door.
The radio alarm comes on,
but as you see
I'm ahead of it, my body-clock
stealing a march –

towards St David's Day,
doing its bit against Zeno as
in league with the machine
the announcer declares
today's the day we realign
with the cosmos.

What planet is she on,
I cry out, where
does she go when off air?
And the hare –
poised to leap into tomorrow
that should have been today.

I can't remember what year
I saw him last near here
like the ghost of John Clare,
nor many another sort
Spring would once
have conjured from its hat

leap year or not,
or turtle dove, or nightjar.
Meanwhile I wait in limbo
for the night,
to see Lepus flee Orion –
and realign me with

Poussie McLièvre
come first of March at last,
Earth on song with chaos
whatever day of the year,
however rigged the calendar
or no calendar at all.

'*O the March Hare! The Hare! / Poussie McLièvre…*' (trad. Scot. late
eighteenth century with fiddle accompaniment), such as granny sang.

NO FIXED ABODE, OR ANOTHER
WILD GOOSE CHASE

i.m. Ian Niall for Jim Perrin

'Not at home, did you say?
And what might you know
about that, I wonder?'
Whose voice was it but
a voice of many more than
anyone can name.

Among them yours
from your hospital deathbed:
'I want to go home,' you said.
Though what did you mean?
A man who'd once belonged
somewhere in childhood.

But me? How can I say
I'm at home or not when
I never was so rooted?
No vagrant of the old school
like Bob in the Whins,
but still of no fixed abode.

Not like those who know
when time's called they have
a home to go to and to leave.
I'm at home only in mind,
to places, folk and times
as they choose to haunt me.

Though still, encumbered by
redundant longing, I seem to think
belonging an ideal state,
a reality beyond my reach –
a trout in a stream
miles away across the *migneint*.

While my mother waits
at the backdoor of her mind
for me to come in, after dark,
wild-eyed and so tired
I can barely stand,
an empty creel in my hand.

migneint: Welsh, meaning 'the rough back place in the bogland'.

HERON

for John Brannigan

See how he unpacks himself
from deep inside his hunger
to stalk, beak-peering,
crest fluttering, freeze-frame
step by step into the same stream twice.

Look, now, where he is,
this object of curiosity,
the handsaw shitepoke,
as he rearranges his anatomy,
reeling in his u-bend neck.

Water is primeval too and
carries itself better, and worse
in the least of drains
and long dry spells
squinting at providence.

See how both reflect –
his head sunk into his shoulders
like a Medieval scribe
who knows our days on earth
are but a shadow.

PLAYING IT BY EAR

What to make of the youth
who hid his violin
in a blackthorn hedge
on the way to school,
after deciding it wasn't for him
and since then
never played a tune
but by ear only?

Was it that he knew
himself – or, less surely,
came and went, guiltily
failing to pluck up courage
to come clean at home?
Or was it both
took up the burden
as life estranged him?

WHEN I WAS GREEN...

When I was green and breaking loose
from what others thought the better course,
my head turned not by paradise
I played the fool to my own interest,
mocking others' middle way of safety-first,
of 'growing up', and knowing best
who never thought of knowing worst
or how rules look when transgressed.
You know the kind of folk I mean,
for God knows what sake erring
on the side of caution, preferring
not to chance their arm, in any name
but toe-the-line, and see this poem
against the grain, that once was green,
as nothing but a waste of time.

NOTES TOWARDS MY OBITUARY

Surviving all mistakes and politics,
reckless adventures, near-death experiences,
betrayals, trespasses, deliverance's lottery,
the nine lives, plus god knows how many.
An on-off affair with the recalcitrant muse.
Both obstinacy and rooted innocence,
all seeming out-of-body in the end:
deathbed gaze, glazed by a window
with a view of estuary and mountain,
a town gasometer like an iron lung; and
gull-haloed waste tip, in seaborne weather,
the westering sun, a distant island.
All as I see them now, from here.
In earshot, the old language of a Nation:
Nonconformist, Welsh hymnal –
so he began, with 'A Short Sermon' and
ironic 'New Dawn', in Welsh backwaters,
supposing he might survive himself,
being, as the young are, immortal.

A LETTER FROM THE WHEELHOUSE

I work my passage. Sometimes these days,
out here, it seems fair to ask
for more art with less matter. But the rub
remains. My mind chafes to wear
the bespoke garment, the officer's rig.
Something nearer off-the-peg,
steerage wear, jeans, tee-shirt
required and yet… (handmade I prefer).
The product of circumstance.
If you like you may call it Providence
and find a moral of your own.

Granny sewed a hank of fishing line
and hooks to last a castaway's lifetime
into the lining of my jacket.
I reckoned I'd do all right on my own –
setting my watch by the tides, and fishing.
Some of those days took as long as a tanker to turn round.
Others ran aground swiftly calling SOS
with all hands lost in an instant.
I was young. I lived the dream I had,
momentarily, and hand-to-mouth
and looked beyond appearances to make ends meet.

I've taken bearing from there ever since.
Voyaging between hard places and rocks,
heart's trials, losses cut, to land catches
too soon tarnished in the day's cold light.
Among my favourite reading
'The Ancient Mariner', *Moby-Dick*, *Crusoe*,
'Le Voyage'… you know the archipelago.

Now and then I go ashore for news
but mostly I turn off the airwaves,
my compass veering from where I am
between 300 and 320 degrees.
Still they get through to me.

You liked X so you might like Y.
Would you recommend 'The Castle Hotel'?
But my heart has an algorithm they've not fathomed.
And I mean to keep it that way.
You can't be too wary to be free of them,
off the map, beyond the satellite.
New deals at Stornoway or Galway
stalk me none the less, 'Genius' offers.
Language doesn't debase itself on its own.
Let storm be shelter. We must go on.
Navigate by the big data of the stars alone.

I admit I wearied long ago of the small anecdote
with a dying fall, pitched too close to prose.
The alternative is not for butterflies
though their true kind know how not to fly to perfection.
Sometimes windborne Brimstone
crossed the Sound to bat the air
as wide as the Atlantic, their timing
beyond all algorithm, a rare species of *rubato*
on the rocks. I tell myself I write for you.
But hard to judge how far to go
knowing a reader and her preferences.

So take this as display. A weather-sign.
A haloed moon. A peacock's eye.
No sooner seen than gone in its own fulfilment.
As I know you, my love, I know

you know what I'm like and how my mind runs weirdly.
Viz. this smudged letter. The albatross also mates for life
and puts in at memory's haven
as when we first fumbled there in the dark.
Whatever life's thrown at the harbour wall
since and will throw, we still meet
over and again, in a world far out beyond
words like resignation or delight.

And you will surely say, 'Sometimes,
these days it seems fair to ask for
more matter with less art.' The rub
remains. I submit my log in private.
Here I just follow my pen and try
to keep leeway enough between
my course and the chart in my head
not that they could ever run akilter.
Knowing when I come back in
you'll read me and know where I am
though I'm not sure until I hold you.

AGAIN

i.m. Arthur Rimbaud

I set sail again –
the territory still there on paper,
as I was, under the skin.

Everything was in order
enough to make my voyage
come close to a return

falling short only by
the usual slippage
between then and now.

And words and words
missing my aim as
they follow their itinerary

with its ports of call,
according to the tide-table –
the moon's cycle –

and all arrangements
made for the elements'
vagaries and variables

and weather permitting,
the forecast for shipping
in the various sea areas

as I ride the hurly-burly,
tossed like a cork from
a bottle with a message in

days and nights away
from the dumb lighthouses,
peninsulas adrift

sea-soar islands aloft,
above, and down below,
the drunken days and nights

of my heart's November.
Warning to bathers
at sewage outlets,

all in my wake,
of *mal de mer* and vomits
as at last I swim free

from here to harbour
by many a metaphor,
in the half-known world –

all returning to me –
until my boat's ashore,
its sail furled.

AS HOME I COME

for Deirdre Ní Chonghaile

If I had the key to time
what would you give me
for the chance to see
Conneely's Guesthouse again
lit up like a liner
on a black night,
as crossing the island
at its narrowest point
home you come
the better for wear?

Oh, I'd give you
the shirt off my back
the boots off my feet
the drink in my glass
to see ruin repaired and
Conneely's Guesthouse
lit up like a liner
on a black night
as home I come
the better for wear.

ST CORNCRAKE'S RETURN

for Lillis Ó Laoire and Cathal Ó Searcaigh

I asked an old man was there
a right of way into the field.
He paused, thinking into English:
'There'd be a little bit of a right of way,
I'd say,' he said. I took him at his word
and slipped in through the gap.

I can't say I was going back.
I was only bringing my Y-chromosome home
hoping to find the drystone wall
my forebears sang
their nightly *aisling* from,
their vigil in sound

through the big small hours.
Crex-crex crex-crex into the cosmos.
Crex-crex crex-crex under the stars.
Sean-Nós between two tides.
The one in the affairs of Man,
the other of the Ocean –

the one I had my money on
playing the long game
as I picked my way through the grass
in the bright karst,
the wind off the sea a whisper
like a sigh before the scythe

before MacCormick's reaper.
I came in like a sleeper
behind enemy lines, waiting
for them to close their eyes
then jammed the airwaves
with my loud-speaker.

Crex-crex crex-crex crex-crex
I gave it to them right and left
visiting the sins of the fathers
on their innocent heads
and the Ocean threatening
to drown them in their beds.

BEYOND THE BREAKER'S YARD

to the M.V. Plassy *for Alex Boyd*

Where most wash up, to look
the hot torch in the eye. Broken
down rivet by rivet, plate by plate,
gutted stern to stem,
all piping, ducts and wiring ripped,
in the rust yard, asset-stripped,
by the carrion executive.

A short history of short lives –
sailor or salvager –
sunk below the waves.
Unless run aground, in the breakers' yard,
barnacle- and limpet-hulled,
an echo-chamber at high tide,
a found poem in the sea's side.

A so-called act of God,
a must for every coastal walker's camera:
chastening witness.
Hope's uninsurable voyage
on its one-way ticket.
Soul refusing to depart.
The poem on its page.

Boat
Sea
Oar
Net
Haul
Hook
Line
Moon
Tide
Neap
Spring
Mountain
Star
Fish
Island
Shore
Wader
Lighthouse
Gull
Gale
Gannet
Skerry
Haven
Harbour
Port
Starboard
Quay
Ferry
Home

A TREASONOUS ACT

*After – a Proclamation, against various 'treasonous acts' by Sir John
Perrot (1528–92), sometime Lord Deputy of Ireland, including
allowing a band of 'northern rhymers' to pass unmolested through
Connacht, when to be a patron of harpers, rhymers, bards, could earn
you the noose. Among such 'northern rhymers' in those days were sever-
al bearing the name Mac an Fhileadh (also recorded as McNeillie /
McNeilly).*

Now join the chase in time –
the wild goose chase
poets have ever lived for,
addicted to word-play and rhyme.

And go from door to door
with your poems to peddle,
doors long ago boarded up
or unhinged to stop a gap

after the horse has bolted
and you astride it with no saddle.
Off to mock all those
who declare themselves good

who'd still have dissenters,
harpers, rhymers, bards –
idlemen and horse-boys –
hung by the neck if they could.

SHIPWRECK

I soon saw whatever craft
I might make of the wreckage,
it could never carry me home.

So I nursed the flame
struck on Vesta's sandpaper hearth
and made what I could of the damage.

The sun told me the time
and the tides divided it
washing Earth's losses ashore.

I foraged by day and wrote at night
in the wide maw of the ocean
as it swallowed the milky way

of krill and plankton.
The starry-eyed hook
at the end of my line a question-mark.

'NEW YEAR'... THE MOVIE

for Diana Maureen Porter

Dissolve or fade, as the screen-writers say,
the old year to start the new.
Let there be flash-backs though
and mystery and revenant moments
haunting every turn of the way,
little clues to say all is not as it seems,
to the observant cinema goer
at the picture palace of dreams.

In this shoot we walk the shore
to blow last night away, to clear
our heads, and poke at what the tide
left on the cutting-room floor,
glistening celluloid fronds of gold
and bronze, miscellaneous dreck,
polystyrene popcorn, and more,
garbage from the ocean's maw.

Let's resolve to solve the riddle
that changes with the weather
and pray Earth gets better.
Though the mistakes come in
with every tide, and truth's a muddle
we tell lies to without knowing
by applying rhyme to reason
in our personal survival bubble.

Where the gaze can say it all,
in a lingering look. O give me
a close-up with you, I say,
as we pause to embrace and turn back,
to a windswept soundtrack.
And give us as many takes
as there's time for, as we co-star
through the dark days ahead.

VISITATION

As when it snows at night
and life's brought to a halt,
the power is out,
lines down, and freezing air
clouds your breath.
Or as, from the storehouse
of dreams, she comes back to you.

Randomly, as she used to be,
as you were both once.
And you ask yourself,
what *are* dreams, and why aren't they
available on demand?
As if for the same reason,
it snows here rarely.

'BOY BITTEN BY A LIZARD'

with apologies to Caravaggio

I dreamt the headline, and wondered where I was,
at what news desk, before what stone,
startled into a long-ago deadline. Had I
lost my mind? I'd been reading about him
when it nipped out towards me from its cranny.
'Man Bites Lizard' blared the *Star* and *Sun*.
But where was I? In what city, on a balcony
with my morning coffee, and the paper
fluttering, like my heart, the biter bit,
remembering an old wall where sudden lizards flashed,
in between the light and dark of sleep,
in the dream's finale, the vital chiaroscuro,
before you went by and looked at me.

LOSS ADJUSTMENT

i.m. Sheila C. McNeillie

1.

No, it's not really in the days
that time takes its toll
but in the nights, mind's
natural element for lunacy;
too late then to bolt
the stable door. Hear it
banging in the storm.
Even this far from
the Atlantic, I hear it.

But daylight also takes a toll,
when I might most hope
to see you or hear you
on the phone, though now
you're gone and reason
tells me, there's no hope
even though it's said
the dead take at least
two lifetimes to die.

2.

'For the principles of loss adjustment
to have any purchase, it's necessary to
establish a liability.' So much for
the analogy, short of 'an insured event'.
Years of wrangling and I have no choice
but bear the cost and write you off
as act of God, or of the gods.
I should have known it. But
it's one thing to know a thing
another to live through it.

When we go to see a Shakespearean tragedy
we know how it will end.
We go to witness the twists and turns of fate
in the name of katharsis and reflection.
But even now when I remember you
and the curtain goes up
I'm still stuck behind the scenes
in endless rehearsal. Enter no one.

No one to the door with
advice on future payments
associated with unpaid claims – or
unpaid losses, loss/claim adjustment
expenses, incurred costs, either
to reclaim or compensate.
No one to walk with by the river.
No Avon lady anymore.

AETAT 16

I know what I need. No smudge
of a poem but a sharp edge.

A summer evening mooched in
the woods of Bodysgallen.

An invisible thrush in a sycamore
singing for no one's pleasure

unless his own. Thunder roaming.
Lightning sizzling. Rain squalling.

And next morning clean as a whistle
of birds at their matins, high treble

call to prayer. World waking.
The day made whole.

And to be forever forsaken
by the girl behind it all.

A DEER

'Truth is forced to fly like a scared white doe in the woodlands;
and only by cunning glimpses will she reveal herself.'
                                        Herman Melville

Mooching through a wood, one day,
I came upon her in all innocence
(if innocence exists, between human and nature)
amazement's chemistry stunning me.
Small birds flitting. The sea not far.
Crow-caw. Gull-mewl. And rain.
Wide-awake, stock-still, she watched me
until she seemed invisible, her form
breaking up like a signal, between branches,
before I realised she wasn't there.

A LITTLE BAGPIPE MUSIC

(i) *The Military Survey of Scotland*
     or Lament for the Mappers

Don't shoot the messenger, for what generals
and their masters commissioned
and pored over, to subjugate
the natives to their will and 'higher
interests' of the State. But treasure
their vision now, and sorrow for its loss,
to Google Earth and lethal GPS,
with a Lament for the Mappers –
their imperfect land-grabs, their use of colour
and shading, their delicate brush-work,
that fade of blue ribbon about the Firth,
the free-hand contours to the North,
the block of green about Culloden House –
who gave us, in the end, an elegy, in love
with what they set out to betray.

(ii) The Golden Fleece
        for Alan Riach

I suppose it's true and fair to say
you've lost the language of your name.
Others had it but couldn't keep
the flame alight; and no blame
on them for being cleared away,
fleeced in the name of sheep.

(iii) Climatology
      after Daniel Defoe 'Letter 13', Northern Scotland

How long since anyone might say of the sea
it was one third water, two-thirds fish?
I don't remember. But so once it was.
As when they came down to Tain they saw
vast shoals of herring milling in the ocean.

It was there too they couldn't understand
a word the people spoke. They might as well
have been in Morocco, he said, and found it
convenient for folk to think they were French…
At least some things haven't changed.

(iv) Spanish (A Squib)
      for Angus Macmillan

Two Lewismen meet up
in a café, in Castle Douglas,
for a little small-language conversation
to comfort their souls.

Four Gallovidian ladies nearby,
exercising their big mouths
in Scots-English, overhear
and are puzzled by the foreign talk.

Until, after listening hard,
one solves the problem
and, in a loud whisper:
'Spanish…' she explains.

WHITEWASHING

I remember how, when I had my part in it,
now long ago (that is, no longer), and lived the life,
in the Republic, hard by the Atlantic,
I reached with my brush at the gable end,
semaphoring, from a world apart –
maybe behind, maybe ahead – in 1969,
as if signalling something in code
before the Troubles really started.

Signifying what? The way quicklime,
where poorly mixed, burns into flesh,
like shrapnel – a sliver
I couldn't wipe away but must haste down
and hurry to the tap, to bride it out,
the wound burning, as grievances burn.

POLDER

I remember the word
and recover it from
my heart's nether lands,
my soul's North Sea
of classroom afternoon
– *ennui* in 'geography'.

I reclaim it, readily,
building dykes of words
on this wide shore,
before it disappears into
the rising tides
of lost knowledge.

DUBLIN POST-CARDS

for Antony Farrell

1. *The River Liffey at Chapelizod*

Here I am, saying again,
'Call me Henry' –
come back by Chapelizod
and keeping my wake awake
by the Liffey, with Farrell,
whose ancestor invented
Porter, and made a killing,
still to be seen drying out,
and dying, by the Liffey.

2. *J. Walsh & Co.'s Pub Stoneybatter*

Forgive me, all of you
who've governed me
from my semi-colonial youth
and pardon my saying:
Henry is my man today –
Henry in the midday court
of Berryman, as opening time
throws time open.
Henry of melancholy
in rain-soaked Ireland.

3. *Arbour Hill Memorial*

Decry the Romantic, if you must,
but once out of the bottle
no modern ever got it
in again (Finnegan),
its mast too tall,
like its stories: the genie
of justice and liberty
too intoxicating… and
(savage indignation)
the visionary paid homage,
too late for all but
martyrdom and elegy.

4. *The North Wall*

I move between *Dream Songs*
Book VII and *Aeneid*
Book VI and read, as I go
Liffey for Styx and vice-
versa-Vico, again, for
another round on me
until time's called and
the dream of life over.

THE OTHER ONE — A SUBURBAN ELEGY

'When one of us dies,' said the old man to his wife,
'I'm going to live in Tipperary.'

But then, he said, it got too late
to clear the house and clear out.
To slip away under cover of darkness
from among the strangers,
the folk called neighbours.

It wasn't one and the same to stay on
and still he longed to be gone.
Though now too late, he knew. His fate
sealed early by the road taken
who should have travelled the other one.

BEYOND JOICE COUNTRY

i.m. Gerald Dawe (1952–2024)

McCharon at the wheel? I hoped not,
though I'd only bought a single,
and so had you. We both made it back,
even so, and time to spare each other,
and all our selves some years,
in-and-out of the *Oscar Wilde*.

How many? I didn't know to wonder.
You were I suppose in remission then,
in chemo's wake. I'd no idea.
You'd kept it to yourself, your other self,
somewhere behind your glasses
in your dream-awake.

There we sat side by side, watching
the West go by, and talking,
switching in and out of the soul's gaze,
gauging distances
by time and speed, and, in your words:
'jabbering about what's past'.

It was Bloomsday, and no coincidence,
chosen to commemorate Richard Murphy,
out there beyond Joice country.
I'd waved goodbye to Nora Barnacle,
the Corrib's torrent, the fishers,
the old sea-road to Inis Mór.

Where Joyce himself once visited
and saw the whitethorn bush
from which Joseph of Arimathea
cut his fabled walking stick.
Had I been there then
we could have swapped walking stick stories

ashplant for ashplant: out there
in my coming of age, my home
from home in monochrome.
But northbound now in the corncrake's month
towards MacNeice's far-near country
and the world of Murphy's lore.

Placenames that overpower me still
from the pages of *Sailing to an Island*:
Letterfrack, Cleggan, Claddaghduff.
Though for all that catches the ear
there's a world and more it can't hear
or the eye see beyond its window.

Stories behind our fellow passengers,
boarding and alighting along the way,
in and out of their souls' eco-systems
at Moycullen, Gortnagroagh, Upper Cloosh –
worlds like plant communities in Roundstone bog,
too deep to know, like time itself.

Like us, figured in our one-inch map
trying to make sense of what's past.
To find a way to write a poem
between subject and object, and
beyond ourselves. The gist of what you said,
in Clifden Church, was Murphy's gift.

The last time I saw you was on Zoom,
a couple of weeks before you died.
You joked about reaching seventy-two.
But of all there was to talk about
you chose our trip beyond Joice Country
and how we'd been absorbed in it.

Now, grievously shaken from my dream-awake,
I don't know what to say.
How to find that place between
subject and object, beyond me,
is beyond me – but yet can't come
between Gerry Dawe and me.

THE OTHER SIDE

Of the many sea-roads that lead there,
there's not a one leads back.

Unless you are the ferryman
who plies from shore to shore.

He has phases of the moon
and tides locked in his DNA

but no idea when your turn
will come, never to return.

No more than you. It might be today.
The weather could be better, I agree.

But at least the storm has gone
and maybe by this afternoon the rain

as the wind goes slack,
sails flap and waves slap

while you stand in line
waiting to disembark.

ANOTHER TIME

> *'For wisdom is the property of the dead,*
> *A something incompatible with life;'*
> W.B. Yeats

I met him you know, another time,
some years later, not many but
I don't remember. If anything,
he seemed more spry, as if he'd
remortgaged himself, extended his lease.
He'd been to the Barbican last night.
'*King Lear*, you know, it seemed appropriate.
I've tickets for *Uncle Vanya* next.
O how Yelena breaks my heart…
How I break my own too. I missed
Lady Macbeth of Mtsensk the other evening.
I'd so looked forward to it but then
I forgot it was on… It happens.
I'm old,' he said, 'you've no idea.'
I had to protest he didn't seem so.
'Old and, of course, irrelevant –
irrelevance the cruellest cross to bear.
DMW – dead man walking.'

Just as before, he was possessed
by work he'd had in hand for months,
some writing, for now he chose
to keep to himself, something
about Tristram and Isolde.
Sadness haunted his gaze, melancholy
of irreparable loss and sorrow.
It hurt to look into his eyes.

Last time he insisted I listen
to Shostakovich's 'Preludes and Fugues'.
This time it was Britten's *War Requiem*,
the final *Libera me* with Owen's 'Strange Meeting'.

'As I say,' he said, 'I am old and
how much longer for the light
is no one's guess. Yet who doesn't
want to go on, to keep hoping?
For what? Peace on Earth?'
He paused, to search a moment.
Then: 'Another victory like that
and we're done for. You remember?
I forget, sometimes. As in a dream,
transitions concealed, leads buried.
I try to pretend it's a rich new vein...
after the fashion of *Finnegans Wake*
but it's harder work, and the jokes
are nowhere near as good.'

He poured us both another dram.

'But I do feel calmer, less impatient,
and if that's wise, so I'm wiser now,
though still I say "wisdom" is for fools.'
(He winked at me, knowingly, aware
I'd heard him say it before.) 'And,
in that, I feel better, and happier
to hear more tenderly the world's song,
to accept what chooses to arrive,
to comfort, bless, or wound again.

But the 24/7 news bombardment?
That's another thing. It lays me waste,
reduces me to rubble. What am I to do?
What does anyone do, obliged to witness
tyranny at work in real time footage?
Real time, unreal time: what's the difference?
Armies fighting, Dead Souls underfoot.
What can we do but signal our virtue
and wring our hands? You tell me.
Sign a letter to the *Times*? I ask you.
March protesting through the streets?
Alas my marching days are behind me.
Or go on hunger strike outside the palace?

I read the *Iliad* for perspective
and go to the play when I can
to see how poorly life imitates art.
I like it most when the curtain falls.
For me that's when the show begins.
The lights come on. The audience
spill onto the street, blinking and
distracted, still bearing witness,
haunted for days afterwards,
adjusting the lighting in their heads,
longing for redress that cannot be.
And on it goes. The National auditions
for another season. Who will play
Tamburlaine? Or Timon? Coriolanus?
Or Gertrude, or Hamlet's uncle –
those trouble-makers behind the throne?'

He shrugged and set his glass down.
Time to send me on my way again.
He talked and walked me to the door,
possessed by his predicament,
refusing to be silent, as if he had
a thing better than silence to say.
Silence, his understudy. *Enter*: A Ghost
impatient for its big break, mouthing an elegy.

So off I went, night-walking home,
no more cast-down than uplifted,
past curtains drawn and undrawn,
lit by screens, here and there a human
crossing a room, looking towards
tomorrow with the usual optimism.

FURNITURE FOR A BARRICADE

'l faut aller fusiller le général Aupick'

The cartographer's 'now' lamplit
in memory of Charles Baudelaire.
Matter yielding to mind,
a world seeming contained.

But no sooner opened from
the origami of its folds
than out fly raven and dove –
moths to the flame of time.

Empires disappearing like Eurydice,
the moment Orpheus turns
or the albatross takes wing
into the South Atlantic air.

What is an old map but a poem
in the theatre of imagination,
an essay in human understanding,
a smudged impression on a seal?

Coast, contour, border, lines merely.
Come and go there as you please
and wander in the wake of your gaze
on the eighth sea of the word.

Trace tales of travel. Tragedy
charting a voyage to the Pole.
Coleridge and Melville passing at sea
in their dark nights of the soul.

History before your eyes relives
mile for a mile, full-scale reality:
footslog from Moscow...
defeat and victory, falling as snow.

The triumph of matter over mind.
Now, mind over matter:
a barricade thrown together,
a doomed gesture, in a tragic time.

CRYING IN THE WILDERNESS

Under cover of night I slip away.
As if anyone will notice, besides me,
though satellites eavesdrop and pry
as they swarm through the stars.

My cursor, a compass needle, veers
to and fro, blinking like a lighthouse
when I pause to check my course.
Don't ask where I'm going or why.

You know well enough, if you know me.
The small hours are filling my sail.
Deeper and deeper into the dark
my metaphor keeps its vigil.

What forecasts there are look bleak
as I go, crying in the wilderness,
with only the wilderness for witness.
Though I cry for the world's sake.

UNLOOKED FOR

It is the unlooked for we look for,
not just the lightning bolt or
coup de foudre but as the heart leaps
at a whisper, finger to lips,
and a nod at a rare creature
on the lawn in hard weather.

The poem of it as brief as a haiku
on a page of new-fallen snow.
Or the melancholy mood swing
between sorrows. A heartfelt song
by an invisible soprano,
soaring from a third-floor window

into a startled summer evening
in a corner of London, a thing
unlooked for that's taken me
off guard again, a reawakened reverie
with its own necessity, as I come
looking now to end a poem

I didn't see coming, nor where
it was going, except down
with the pull of gravity,
swinging from rhyme to rhyme,
a drunken pendulum
in a long clock like a coffin.

ACKNOWLEDGEMENTS

For the term 'A Wild Goose Chase', in its reputedly original equestrian context, see Gervase Markham's manual *The Hunter: A Discourse of Horsemanship* (1593).

'In the Wake of Pytheas' first appeared in *Poetry Wales* and I am most grateful to Zöe Brigley that it did. The poem owes its inspiration (and much else of 'fact') to Barry Cunliffe's *The Extraordinary Voyage of Pytheas the Greek. The man who discovered Britain* (Penguin, 2001).

The setting for the poem 'Edge-ways' is, or was, O'Dowd's pub by Roundstone harbour, in Connemara. (It is thus based on licensed premises, in both senses of the term, as Myles na gCopaleen would say.) The book referred to in the poem is Tim Robinson's *Setting Foot on the Shores of Connemara* (Lilliput, 1996). The poem's title nods (and no more) at 'The World Seen Edgeways', the first subtitle in Robinson's essay 'The Curvature of the Earth', published in *My Time in Space* (Lilliput, 2001). The poem, accompanied by a short essay, is to be included in a collection of tributes to the late Tim Robinson, edited by Patrick Curry and John Drever for the Lilliput Press. It was originally published, with others here, in *Poetry Salzburg Review*.

'Singing School' owes much to *Melville's Bibles* (2008) by Ilana Pardes and to a lifetime's fascination with *Moby-Dick* itself.

Some of the poems have appeared in Robert Selby's *Wild Court*, in the *TLS* and (additionally, beyond the 'Pytheas' poem) in *Poetry Wales*. 'Loch Scavaig from Elgol' was written to address the etching of that title by Jason Hicklin as part of his 'Skye Box Set. The Vast Silence', launched at the Eames Gallery in Bermondsey, in January 2026. 'Norman Ackroyd's Nightwatch' was published in *Archipelago 2:4*, an issue dedicated to his memory.